ORANG-UTAN
Órang-Útan

Gabriel Rosenstock

© Gabriel Rosenstock 2025
Layout by Mandy Marcus

ORANG-UTAN
Órang-Útan

New & selected haiku for older children with a stunning gallery of international art

"Orangoetan" (1914)
Samuel Jessurun de Mesquita (1868–1944)

Preface

Artwork used in this book of haiku and senryū for older children falls under Public Domain or Fair Use, i.e. artwork that is widely available on the internet, on such platforms as Artvee, Wikicommons and Wikiart.
Thanks also to the artists who gave permission to use the artwork.

~

Senryū look like haiku but are intended as playful squibs. Indeed, haiku were essentially playful compositions until great depth was added to them by such Japanese grandmasters as Bashō, Chiyo-ni, Issa, Buson, Shiki and Santōka. Later, in the 20th century, haiku masters and haiku organisations came to the fore in dozens of countries throughout the world.

~

It's best to **dip** into haiku books, such as this one, rather than read them from cover to cover. In fact, haiku is an awakening experience so if you stop reading and then read the same haiku a week later, you might experience something else entirely! So, were you asleep a week ago, or are you asleep now?!

~

The texts in *Orang-Utan* range from the lyrical to the contemplative, the questioning to the absurd, and are suitable for readers 10–14+.

Gabriel Rosenstock

Henri Martin (An Fhrainc / *France*)

an seolann siad leo
chuig cuan sábháilte?
aislingí ár n-óige

do they sail away
to some safe harbour?
dreams of our youth

Karl Wiener (An Ostair / *Austria*)

is iomaí
cruth a bhíonn orthu . . .
púcaí-schmúcaí

they come
in many shapes and forms . . .
spookie-wookies!

Jean-Léon Gérôme (An Fhrainc / *France*)

bhíodh an-ghá aige
le dreas maith codlata . . .
Naomh Iaróm

he was often in need
of a decent nap . . .
St. Jerome

Alexander Koester (An Ghearmáin / *Germany*)

a lachain
ná bígí in bhur suí ansin!
tá doineann air

ducks
don't just sit there!
a storm is brewing

Philip de László (An Ungáir & An Bhreatain / *Hungary & Britain*)

cuimhne iasc órga
cúig shoicind? cúig mhí?
ní cuimhin liom

    memory span of a goldfish
    five seconds? five months?
    I forget

Nicolae Grigorescu (An Rómáin / *Romania*)

cén fáth a bhfuil tú ag stánadh?
éirigh as . . .
scanróidh tú an ghé

why are you staring?
stop staring . . .
you will frighten my goose

Jules Bastien-Lepage (An Fhrainc / *France*)

Díoiginéas is a lampa
duine cóir fós
á lorg aige

> *Diogenes with his lamp*
> *still searching*
> *for an honest man*

Jan Ciągliński (An Pholainn / *Poland*)

ár mbuíochas as a bheith
mar atá tú . . .
i d'fhuinneog

    thank you
    for being what you are . .
    a window

Käthe Kollwitz (An Ghearmáin / *Germany*)

ná bíodh cogadh arís ann!
abair é . . .
abair gach lá é

no more war!
say it . . .
say it every day

Richard Dadd (An Bhreatain / *Britain*)

deir siad anois
gur caipitlí lofa a bhí ionat . . .
Robin Hood

now they say
you were another filthy capitalist . . .
Robin Hood

Mikuláš Galanda (An tSlóvaic / *Slovakia*)

grá!
leáfaidh an domhan go léir
i ngrá

love!
the whole world will dissolve
in love

Eugène Joseph Verboeckhoven (An Bheilg / *Belgium*)

imeoidh tú uaim
lá éigin, a uainín . . .
ach ní go fóill, ní go fóill

some day
you'll leave me, little lamb . . .
not yet, not yet

Lee Campbell (An Nua-Shéalainn & Sasana / *New Zealand & England*)

dhá chruidín . . .
má fheiceann siad iasc
cén ceann is túisce ina dhiaidh?

two kingfishers . . .
if they spot a fish
which one's the first to dive?

Karl Wiener (An Ostair / *Austria*)

i bhfolach arís
laistiar den chnoc is ansa leat?
ré oráiste

> *were you hiding*
> *behind your favourite hill again?*
> *orange moon*

Paul Klee (An Eilvéis & An Ghearmáin / *Switzerland & Germany*)

cad eile a bheadh uait?
. . . balún dearg

who would want anything more?
. . . red balloon

Jakob Smits (An Bheilg / *Belgium*)

an phóg
ab fhuaire riamh –
póg Iúdáis

coldest kiss
of all –
the kiss of Judas

Joseph Decker (An Ghearmáin & SAM / *Germany & USA*)

an cailín béal dorais . . .
na súile aici ar dhath
plumaí glasa

> *the girl next door . . .*
> *her eyes the colour*
> *of green plums*

Johann Friedrich Naumann (An Ghearmáin / *Germany*)

tá rud éigin
ag titim amach . . .
tá's ag na rúcaigh é

something's going on . . .
the rooks know
all about it

Eero Järnefelt (An Fhionlainn / *Finland*)

cuma an-uaigneach orthu . . .
cosa préacháin
i linn

    they seem
    so terribly alone . . .
    crowfeet in a pond

Eanger Irving Couse (SAM / *USA*)

Cos Eilce
a leithéid d'ainm!
hé, a leithéid d'ainm!

Elk Foot
what a name!
hey, what a name!

Edmund Blair Leighton (An Bhreatain / *Britain*)

a stail amadáin!
imigh leat is iompaigh d'armúr
ina chéachta

foolish man!
go and make a plough
of your armour

Franz von Stück (An Ghearmáin / *Germany*)

choinníodh sé
an pota fuail faoin bpianó aige . . .
Beethoven

he kept his chamber pot
under the piano . . .
Beethoven

Epifanio Fuentes Vázquez (Meicsiceo / *Mexico*)

seans nach gcreideann tú iontu
ach creideann siadsan ionatsa . . .
aingil

> *you may not believe in them*
> *but they believe in you . . .*
> *angels*

Julie de Graag (An Ollainn / *Holland*)

ní gá ordú a thabhairt dó . . .
níonn an cat
é féin

without being told
to do so . . .
the cat washes himself

Tadeusz Makowsky (An Pholainn / *Poland*)

tá séitéir cártaí
ina measc . . .
ach cén duine acu é, n'fheadar?

there's a cardsharp
among them . . .
but which fella is it?

Christian Rohlfs (An Ghearmáin / *Germany*)

a Mhaois! tír ina mbeadh
bainne is mil ina slaoda
do chách?

*Moses! what about a land
of milk and honey
for all?*

Harald Sohlberg (An Iorua / *Norway*)

faolchúnna stiúgtha . . .
ocras ar a gcuid scáthanna
fiú

hungry wolves . . .
even their shadows
are starving

Ewald Rübsaamen (An Ghearmáin / *Germany*)

ESCAPED
octopus: if spotted,
ring Aquarium!

AR IARRAIDH
ochtapas: má fheiceann tú é
glaoigh ar an Uisceadán!

Asai Chū (An tSeapáin / *Japan*)

cuilithíní . . .
a bhfoinse á lorg
ag froganna

ripples . . .
frogs in search
of their source

(Ealaín Ionúiteach / *Inuit art*)

níl a fhios agat cad atá ionam
is úcpic mé:
ulchabhán!

    you don't even know
    what I am: I'm an ookpik
    an ookpik! an owl!

Ilmari Aalto (An Fhionlainn / *Finland*)

na Fianna –
ceol na gclog
leo níor bhinn

*the Fianna –
ancient warriors of Ireland –
church bells drove them mad*

Eugenie Bandell (An Ghearmáin / *Germany*)

á!
plaic a bhaint as úll . . .
brionglóid na bábóige

ah!
to bite into an apple . . .
a doll's dream

Leonetto Cappiello (An Iodáil / *Italy*)

an maith leat súp?
is maith?
knorr laga dia thú!

do you like soup?
no? no
nor I!

Eugen von Blaas (An Ostair & An Iodáil / *Austria & Italy*)

cén fáth a n-imíonn siad?
an bhfillfidh siad go deo?
fáinleoga

> *why do they leave?*
> *will they return?*
> *swallows*

(Ealaín Ionúiteach / *Inuit art*)

lig dom
led' thoil
ceart go leor?

    just leave me be
    OK?
    OK?

Charles Edouard Delort (An Fhrainc / *France*)

an t-uafás rudaí
ag déanamh scime dhó . . .
cairdinéal

so many things
on his mind . . .
the cardinal

Eero Järnefelt (An Fhionlainn / *Finland*)

scamallóireacht . . .
in áit an ailgéabair?
más é do thoil é!

*cloud gazing . . .
instead of algebra?
yes, please!*

Klemens Brosch (An Ostair / *Austria*)

Mugo wa Kibiru, fáidh,
chonaic sé an Nathair Iarainn
ag teacht!

*Mugo wa Kibiru, seer,
he saw the coming
of the Iron Snake!*

Nicolas Toussaint Charlet (An Fhrainc / *France*)

maidin i nGoa . . .
dúisíonn dreancaidí strae
ar mhadraí strae

morning in Goa . . .
stray fleas waking up
on stray dogs

Gwen John (An Bhreatain Bheag / *Wales*)

cat darbh ainm Edgar
ar iarraidh
ón mbliain 1908

> *a cat*
> *by the name of Edgar*
> *missing since 1908*

Konstantinos Volanakis (An Ghréig / *Greece*)

lig dom taisteal leat!
long ag seoladh
trí néalta

      take me on board!
      ship sailing
      through clouds

Stefan Luchian (An Rómáin / *Romania*)

léi féin lena cuid smaointe
is leis na blátha . . .
cailín na mbláth

alone with her thoughts
and her flowers . . .
flower seller

August Malmström (An tSualainn / *Sweden*)

mall
ar nós na scamall . . .
amhráin na sean

movement of clouds
songs of the ancients . . .
slow

Isidor Kaufmann (An Ungáir / *Hungary*)

tá sé ag teacht go deas
leis an hata fionnaidh . . .
clúmh aghaidhe an raibí

it matches
his fur hat nicely . . .
the rabbi's facial hair

Kawanabe Kyōsai (An tSeapáin / *Japan*)

má thugann sé claonfhéachaint ort
tabhair claonfhéachaint ar ais air –
préachán

if he looks at you sideways
look sideways back at him –
crow

Tadeusz Makowski (An Pholainn / *Poland*)

tá cuma na holla
ag teacht ar a fhéasóg . . .
an t-aoire maith

*his beard
is turning into fleece* . . .
the good shepherd

Nikolaos Gyzis (An Ghréig / *Greece*)

níl sé baileach
chomh maith is a bhíodh . . .
bearbóir ag dul in aois

not quite the man
he once was . . .
ageing barber

Shitao (An tSín / *China*)

gach éinne is gach aon ní
ag dul in aois . . .
carraig fiú amháin

everything and everybody
growing older . . .
even a rock

Hoca Ali Riza (An Tuirc / *Turkey*)

fásann sé ar chrann
tá a fhios agat . . .
an phiostáis

        they grow on trees
        you know . . .
        pistachios

William James Webbe (An Bhreatain / *Britain*)

cad atá
ar an taobh eile den chnoc?
tá tuairim ag an gcamall

what lies
beyond the next hill?
the camel is guessing

Maurice Pillard Verneuil (An Fhrainc / *France*)

'bhfuil do pharaisiút slán?
ioraí rua! ag caint
ar a n-eireaball

is your parachute working?
squirrels! always talking
about their tail

José Garnelo (An Spáinn / *Spain*)

rud uaigneach é . . .
an pianó
nach seinntear

lonely thing . . .
unplayed
piano

Franz von Defregger (An Ostair / *Austria*)

caith cleite . . .
ní bheadh a fhios agat
cad a thitfeadh amach

wear a feather . . .
you never know
what might happen

Johann Friedrich Naumann (An Ghearmáin / *Germany*)

rat-a-tat-tat
nach dtagann tuirse riamh air?
mórchnagaire breac

rat-a-tat-tat
does it never get tired?
great spotted woodpecker

Claude Monet (An Fhrainc / *France*)

gan aon choinne aige
leis an sneachta . . .
snag breac balbh

stunned
by the snow . . .
the magpie is speechless

Vincent van Gogh (An Ollainn / *Holland*)

is cuma leis
cá bhfuil a thriall . . .
féileacán

it doesn't care
where it's going . . .
butterfly

Yamamoto Sodō (An tSeapáin / *Japan*)

cleitearnach sciathán . . .
dlúthchairde freisin
ní mór dóibh scaradh

flutter of wings . . .
even the best of friends
must part

Constantin Artachino (An Rómáin / *Romania*)

an nuacht:
an lá inné ag éag
splanc ag dul as

the news:
yesterday is dying
vanishing spark

Henriëtte Ronner-Knip (An Ollainn & An Bheilg / *Holland & Belgium*)

cara
á lorg . . .
déanfaidh luch an chúis

playmate
wanted . . .
a mouse will do

Walter Greaves (An Bhreatain / *Britain*)

"heileo?
ar lig duine éigin fead?"
arsa James McNeill Whistler

*"hello?
did someone just whistle?"
asks James McNeill Whistler*

Jacques Louis David (An Fhrainc / *France*)

Comte Henri-Amédée-Mercure
De Turenne-D'aynac –
ainm fada!

*Comte Henri-Amédée-Mercure
De Turenne-D'aynac –
long name!*

Edouard Manet (An Fhrainc / *France*)

"bímis inár ndlúthchairde
go deo deo!"
an chéad chara a bhí agam

*"let's be besties
always! always!"
my first friend*

Utagawa Hiroshige (An tSeapáin / *Japan*)

imigh leat
nó anraith searbh a bheidh ionat!
sclamhaire dearg

go away
or you'll end up as sour soup!
red snapper

Victor Hugo (An Fhrainc / *France*)

cén ceol
lena bhfuil sé ag éisteacht?
ochtapas ag damhsa

what music
is it listening to?
dancing octopus

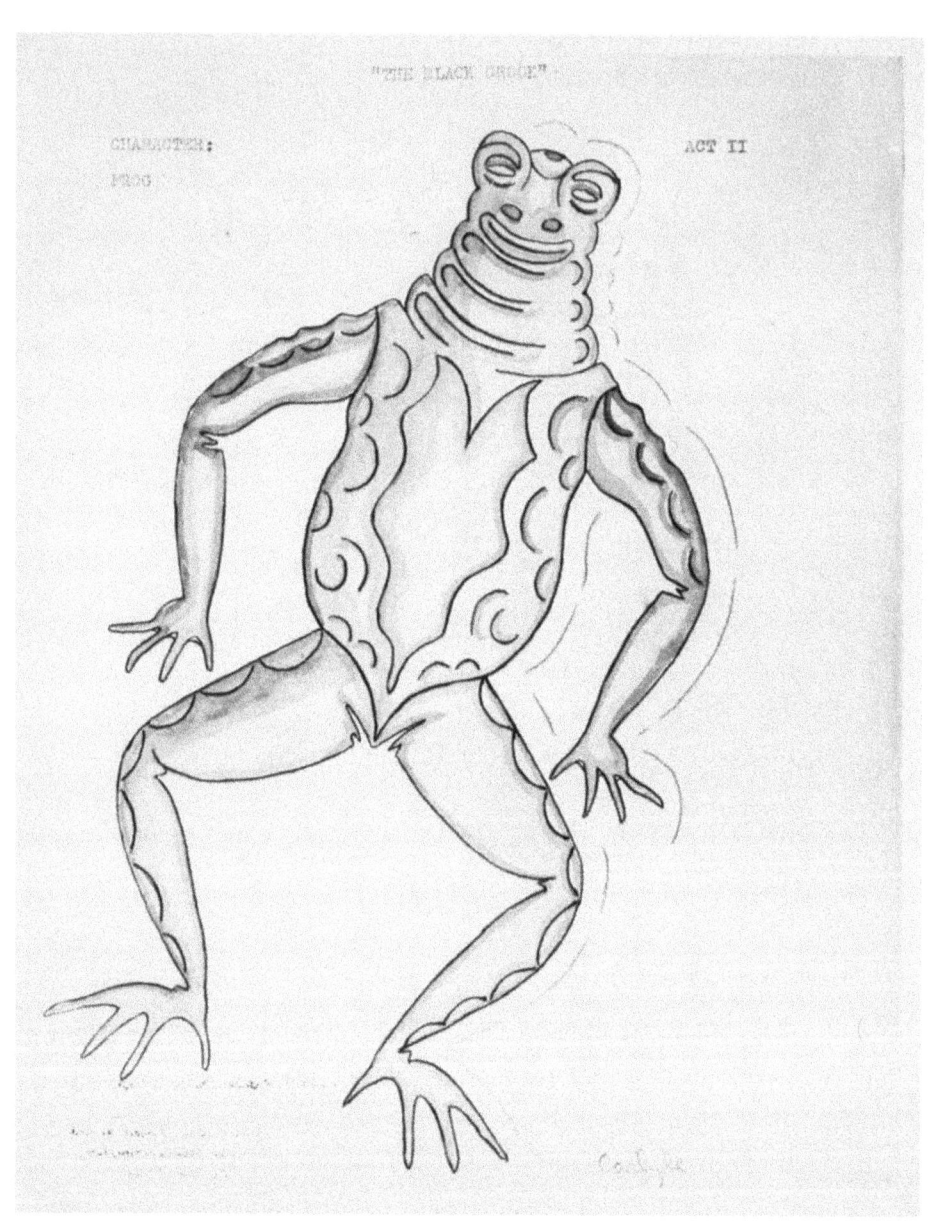

Sidney Carlyle (SAM / *USA*)

arsa an frog leis féin –
cad tá cearr le daoine?
cén fáth nach bpreabann siad?

the frog thinks –
what's wrong with people?
why don't they hop?

Moriz Jung (An Ostair / *Austria*)

ba thapúla é tráth
ná gaoth an Mhárta . . .
cú

he once outraced
the March wind . . .
greyhound

Stanhope Forbes (Éire & An Bhreatain / *Ireland & Britain*)

Mousehole
i gCorn na Breataine –
'Muzal' a deirtear!

*Mousehole –
a town in Cornwall
pronounced 'Muzzle'!*

Gerrit Willem Dijsselhof (An Ollainn / *Holland*)

éisc
is aislingigh iad . . .
iad go léir léir

> *fish*
> *daydreamers . . .*
> *the whole lot of them*

Honoré Daumier (An Fhrainc / *France*)

an ceol a dhéanann bonn
ag titim ar bhonn . . .
ceoltóirí sráide

the music of a coin
falling on a coin . . .
buskers

Giulio Aristide Sartorio (An Iodáil / *Italy*)

seandealbha
ag iarraidh labhairt linn . . .
cé a thuigeann iad?

old statues
trying to speak to us . . .
who knows what they're saying?

Hocine Ziani (An Ailgéir / *Algeria*)

cruálacht gach áit . . .
an ghealach féin
ag teitheadh chun na hÉigipte

cruelty everywhere . . .
look! even the moon
is hastening to Egypt

Raja Ravi Varma (An India / *India*)

ceannaigh
d'airnéis Mháisiúnach anois
fad is atá sí i stoc!

> *while stocks last . . .*
> *get your Masonic regalia*
> *now!*

Archibald Thorburn (Albain / *Scotland*)

a chreabhair
coinnigh do ghob dúnta . . .
plúchadh sneachta!

woodcock
keep your beak shut . . .
it's a blizzard!

Eugène Jansson (An tSualainn / *Sweden*)

gan soilse
á dtreorú . . .
aimsíonn tonnta an trá

no lights
to guide them . . .
yet waves find a shore

James Abbott McNeill Whistler (SAM / *USA*)

duine éigin
(ní fios cé hé)
ag trasnú Dhroichead Battersea

somebody
(nobody knows who)
crossing Battersea Bridge

Paul Goesch (An Ghearmáin / *Germany*)

mharaigh Earcail leon . . .
chuirfí i bpríosún
inniu é

> *Hercules killed a lion . . .*
> *he'd be arrested for it*
> *today*

Hashimoto Kansetsu (An tSeapáin / *Japan*)

ceolfhoireann dhofheicthe
á stiúradh aige –
giobún

conducting
an invisible orchestra –
the gibbon

Konstantin Korovin (An Rúis / *Russia*)

líon na scáthanna
gan áireamh a ghabh tríd . . .
Páras

the countless shadows
that have passed through . . .
Paris

Knud Baade (An Iorua / *Norway*)

saoirse na sairdíní
sula gcuirtear iad go léir
i gcannaí

    the freedom
    of sardines
    before they're all canned

Jan Mankes (An Ollainn / *Holland*)

cad tá ar eolas aige
nach eol dúinne?
ligeann an préachán scréach

he knows something
that we don't . . .
screaming crow

Paul Henry (Éire / *Ireland*)

titeann an oíche
ar an ngliomadóir . . .
is ar na gliomaigh

night falls
on the lobster fisher . . .
and on the lobsters

Samin Sammoun (An Liobáin & Ceanada / *Lebanon & Canada*)

lá ceo
cuma thréigthe
ar Nua-Eabhrac

foggy day
New York
looks deserted

Winslow Homer (SAM / *USA*)

a lár bhán . . .
tabhair leat sinn
ar scamall bán

white mare . . .
take us with you
on a white cloud

Ohara Koson (An tSeapáin / *Japan*)

ní fhaca
an t-iasc ag teacht é . . .
cruidín

the fish
never saw him coming . . .
kingfisher

Helene Schjerfbeck (An Fhionlainn / *Finland*)

cad as ar tháinig siad?
an Spáinn? an Iodáil?
líomóidí i mbabhla

where did they come from?
Spain? Italy?
lemons in a bowl

John Frederick Herring Snr (An Bhreatain / *Britain*)

luch bhán
á lorg aige ar feadh a shaoil . . .
cat bán

all its life
in search of a white mouse . . .
white cat

John Lavery (Tuaisceart Éireann / *Northern Ireland*)

cailleadh iad
de bharr píosa éadaigh . . .
bratach

    they died
    all for a piece of cloth . . .
    a flag

William Orpen (Éire / *Ireland*)

cabaireacht bhialainne . . .
gliomach beo á chur
in uisce fiuchaidh

restaurant chatter . . .
a live lobster placed
in boiling water

Gabriel von Max (An Ostair / *Austria*)

in Goa
ciallaíonn *tu magel moga cho*
'*tá grá agam duit!*'

    in Goa
    '*tu magel moga cho*'
    means, 'I love you!'

Isaac van Ostade (An Ollainn / *Holland*)

muc (gan ainm) . . .
ar iarraidh ón mbliain
1645

      pig (no name) . . .
      missing since
      1645

Lemuel Maynard Wiles (SAM / *USA*)

féach thart . . .
cé atá saor?
cé atá i gcarcair?

       look around . . .
       who is free?
       who is imprisoned?

Cyprián Majernik (An tSlóvaic / *Slovakia*)

is tusa iad
is mise . . .
teifigh

> *they are you*
> *they are me . . .*
> *refugees*

Serhi Svetoslavsky (An Úcráin / *Ukraine*)

cúpla storc . . .
froganna aimsithe acu
de réir dealraimh

a couple of storks . . .
looks like they've found
some frogs

Interlude: Haiku for a Rainy Day

Do you like rain? For some it's an annoyance. For others, it's a blessed gift, or a dire necessity. Without rain, there would be no rice harvest in Japan, for instance, where farmers call rain tensui, 'water of Heaven'.

In Ireland, we get buckets of rain, coming in from the Atlantic and, so, in the senior language, Irish, we have lots of words for rain: *Báisteach* (or *Báisleach*), often heavy rain; *Bailc*, a downpour; *Brádarnach*, a slight fall; *Braoille*, a heavy shower; the phrase *an braon anuas* is 'rain coming in through the roof'; the phrase *lá breac-fhliuch* means 'a day with occasional showers'; *Clagarnach*, the sound of heavy rain; *Claimhreach gabhair* (literally goat's hair) describes ragged clouds that are bringing rain; *Ceathach* or *caothach*, an adjective meaning showery; *Cith* is a shower and so is *múr* or *smúr*; *Ceathán* a light shower; *Frais-chioth* is another word for a light shower; *Gailbh*, a light shower with wind; *Scrabha*, a passing shower; *Toinn-chith*, a violent shower.

If you see *Corrghogailt* when raking the fire at night – ghostly blue and green figures – you can expect rain the following day; *Draoghnán*, a drizzle; *Raiste*, furious rain, driven by the wind; *Siabh-fhearthainn*, small rain with wind; *Fuarlach báistí*, torrential rain; *Lascadh báistí*, slashing rain . . . and so on. Some of these words are becoming archaic and seldom used. No doubt, some will become obsolete.

There used to be innumerable sayings about rain, many of them no longer heard in our era of increasing monoculture. If your shadow appears bigger than usual, a sign of rain! When the cat sits with her back to the fire, a sign of rain – or when she washes behind her ears! If the animals go to sleep early, you can bet that rain is on the way. If there's mist on the mirror, if the blackbird changes its song, if a dog bites the grass . . . when a lone curlew cries . . . the list goes on and on. One could write a book about it. And that's exactly what I did. It's called *Irish Weather Wisdom: Signs of Rain* (Appletree Press, 2000).

~

The Japanese haiku master Kobayashi Issa (1763 -1828) – like most haiku poets – welcomed rain. Why not? What would be the point of not welcoming rain . . . or snow, or wind, or sunshine?

All types of weather are welcomed by a haiku master, all kinds of events become part of her/his haiku life. That's the way it is. The way of haiku. The way of grateful acceptance.

Issa often sees the humour in a situation. In the year 1814 he had a lame chicken hobbling around the place. The chicken decides to go for a stroll but as soon as it puts its head outside the door, it is greeted by an icy, wintry shower, poor thing. This is one of the rain haiku found below, humour mixed with compassion.

OK, maybe Issa shows his annoyance with rain now and again but his annoyance feeds into his haiku diary, the record of his own life which is simply a witnessing of the world and of himself.

Of course, he lived before the Industrial Revolution, before the hard rain of climate change would turn everything upside down. Maybe we'll get it right again.

préacháinín
nach cliste mar a sciorr sé . . .
báisteach earraigh

baby crow
how cleverly he has just slipped . . .
Spring rain

báisteach earraigh
an luch is mé féin
ar ár suaimhneas

soft rain . . .
me and the mouse
taking it nice and easy

fearthainn . . .
calóga sneachta tríthi
anois is arís

it's not all rain . . .
here and there
snowflakes flutter

plup-plap
an ghealach i mbraonta báistí . . .
géanna fiáine ag imeacht

drip-drip
moon-filled raindrops . . .
wild geese departing

Issa would have loved this beautiful depiction of an egret in rain by his fellow-countryman Ohara Koson (1877-1945). Let us try to compose an Issa-like haiku, in response to Koson's image:

>   díreach anuas a thagann sí
>   féachann an éigrit ar chlé:
>   dianfhearthainn

>   *straight down it comes*
>   *and the egret looks to the left . . .*
>   *hard rain*

Haiku is not some fly stuck forever in amber, a changeless thing. It can incorporate a limitless amount of references, such as Bob Dylan's 'hard rain' above.

And haiku should come as naturally as rain. If you get into the haiku habit, haiku can be composed spontaneously. Back now to Isa's rain haiku:

garsún óg
coca beag féir ar a dhroim . . .
báisteach shamhraidh

*a little boy
a bundle of hay on his back . . .
summer rain*

scairteann scréachán . . .
locháin ar an mbóithrín
ag trá

*a shrike calls out . . .
rain puddles along the boreen
drying up*

tá an colúr sléibhe
ag gearán arís . . .
báisteach gheimhridh

*he's complaining again . . .
mountain pigeon
in winter rain*

meirg ar laiste an dorais
dearg dorcha . . .
báisteach gheimhridh

    rust on the door latch
    a deep red . . .
    winter rain

báisteach gheimhridh . . .
an sicín bacach
ag siúl ar éigean

    winter rain . . .
    the bockety chicken
    dragging its leg

scamaill bholgtha . . .
is dubh iad na sléibhte
faoin mbáisteach

    billowing clouds . . .
    a mountain in rain
    black as ink

aer fionnuar . . .
gearrann tintreach
tríd an mbáisteach

cool air . . .
lightning slices
through a shower of rain

an féar báite ag an mbáisteach
gealach sa ghiúis . . .
géanna ag imeacht

rain has drenched the grass
the moon sits in the pine . . .
wild geese leaving

Rain can be a dramatic event, as we see in this painting by John Constable:

Great painters such as Constable, and great haijin (haiku masters) such as Issa, awaken us to the drama of rain.

It's such a tragedy! Many people fall asleep as soon as art or poetry is mentioned: one of the purposes of the arts – especially haiku – is to keep us awake to the gifts of life. And rain is one of them. I have heard of rich Arabs flying to Mumbai to witness the great downpour known as the monsoon.

Give yourself a treat! Listen to the choral group Ladysmith Black Mambazo singing *Rain, Rain, Beautiful Rain*.

ligeann grág as
is léimeann san fhéar fliuch . . .
leipreachán an chlaí *

    he croaks
    then leaps out of his skin . . .
    *leprechaun of the ditch **

                             * *frog*

fágann an ghaoth
muinchille amháin díom fuar . . .
báisteach fhómhair

    one sleeve
    chilled by the wind . . .
    autumn rain

a ghob ar oscailt
ag feitheamh lena mháthair
gearrcach faoin mbáisteach fhómhair

    its beak open
    waiting for mother . . .
    a nestling in autumn rain

é lán d'imní
trí na braonta fearthainne . . .
féileacán earraigh

anxiously flitting
among raindrops . . .
Spring butterfly

leath i bhfolach
faoi chith fearthainne . . .
bláthanna silíní

shower of rain . . .
cherry blossoms
barely visible

cuireann báisteach um thráthnóna
ag canadh é . . .
dreoilín

evening shower . . .
he bursts into song
little wren

fear bréige
ag breathnú orm . . .
fearthainn fhuar

    a scarecrow
    looking at me . . .
    icy rain

tar isteach
fan liomsa, a sheilide . . .
báisteach gheimhridh tosaithe

    come inside
    live with me, wee snail . . .
    winter rain begins

Issa is renowned for his love of little creatures such as insects and fleas which many of us ignore or shy away from.

OK, here we go again: I'll compose a spontaneous haiku now in that same spirit of Issa, this time in response to an artist from my own part of the world, Norman Garstin, born in Co. Limerick:

**chualadar an bháisteach ag teacht –
seangáin is feithidí
i bhfolach**

*they heard the rain coming –
ants and insects
in hiding*

Try writing spontaneous haiku of your own in response to artwork. Once you've got it down, you can polish it whenever you feel like it. Look at your haiku. Maybe the lines are in the wrong order? Maybe it could be tightened a bit (without choking it).

You can follow the 5-7-5 syllable pattern (17 syllables) or else a haiku of 12 or so syllables. Here's a book that might be helpful:

A few more rain haiku from Issa:

> báisteach earraigh –
> vác-vác na lachan
> nár itheadh fós

> *spring rain –*
> *quack-quack!*
> *uneaten ducks . . .*

> teastaíonn ón sicín bacach
> bualadh amach . . . hoips!
> bailc gheimhridh

> *the bockety chicken*
> *decides to go out . . . oops!*
> *sudden winter shower*

báisteach earraigh
ar dhuilleog bhambú . . .
á lí ag luch

little pool of Spring rain
on a bamboo leaf . . .
a mouse licks it

i lár na báistí fuaire
dall óg
ag lorg deirce

in the middle
of a ceaseless winter downpour . . .
a young blind beggar

plap!
titeann braon baistí . . .
cuimlíonn buaf a ceann

plop!
a raindrop falls . . .
the toad rubs his head

I'll write one more haiku inspired by Ohara Koson and the sensitive spirit of Issa:

néalta dubha . . .
díríonn an naoscach
ar fhoinse na báistí

dark clouds . . .
the snipe points
to the rain's source

If you enjoyed some of Issa's rain haiku, you will surely enjoy his snow haiku as well:

Iarfhocal / Afterword

Why is this book called *Orang-Utan*? For no other reason than that I like the face of the orang-utan as depicted by Dutch artist Samuel Jessurun de Mesquita.

The animal is quietly minding his own business, grooming himself, and looks friendlier than a lot of people I know. Orang-utan is a Malay word: *orang* means 'a person' and *hutan* means 'a forest'.

One of the countries associated with the orang-utan is Borneo. I was a bit wild as a boy and my mother called me 'The Wild Man from Borneo'. Was I pleased with the name? Yes.

Believe it or not, some haiku masters in Japan say that to write haiku one must be a little wild, a little crazy. Many of them were eccentric. Poets such as Ryokan didn't care about society and its rules. Ryokan wanted what is called in Zen-Buddhism, 'the beginner's mind' and as far as he was concerned, most adults had lost that. He preferred the company of children, and *found* himself (so to speak!), or rediscovered his 'original mind', when playing hide-and-seek with them.

A modern Zen master, Shunryu Suzuki, tells us:

> "If your mind is empty, it is always ready for anything; it is open to everything. In the beginner's mind there are many possibilities; in the expert's mind there are few . . ."

What has this got to do with haiku? Everything! And not just haiku. All the arts benefit greatly from the beginner's mind. Suzuki again:

> "This is also the real secret of the arts: always be a beginner . . ."

~

Traditional haiku dealt with keen observations and little adventures over the course of five seasons, Spring, Summer, Autumn, Winter and New Year. They were and still are mainly nature-centred. Modern haiku (gendai haiku) can deal with any subject. The book you are reading now, *Orang-Utan*, has been influenced by classic haiku and gendai haiku alike.

~

Who is our cover artist, Samuel Jessurun de Mesquita? I had never heard of him before coming across his wonderful orang-utan. He was Jewish-Dutch of Portuguese descent. I was shocked to discover that he was one of the millions who perished during the Holocaust. A Sephardic Jew, he was an old man, his health failing, when the Nazis arrived on the morning of the 1st February, 1944, to pack him off to Auschwitz. He and his wife were gassed there. The horror is inconceivable.

Their son, Jaap, was sent to another concentration camp where he, too, was put to death.

Maybe we should step down and put orang-utans in charge of the show. What say you? Actually, a novel by the delightfully named Thomas Love Peacock, *Melincourt* (1817), features Sir Oran Haut Ton, an orang-utan who becomes a candidate for the British Parliament!

~

The Dutch seem to be particularly gifted as draughtsmen and de Mesquita taught some of the best of them, including M. C. Escher, who said in an interview that he visited his beloved master during the hungry winter of 1944:

> I wanted to bring them something, apples . . .
> I entered their house. The windows on the first floor were broken. The neighbours said: "Did you not hear? The de Mesquitas have been taken away."

~

A few of my children's books (which I wrote in Irish) were illustrated by multi-talented Dutchmen who had come to live in Ireland, Piet Sluis (1929 -2008) and Gerrit van Gelderen (1926 -1994).

A third Dutchman, Leo Bosch, was a naïve artist and one of the funniest men I ever came across. He often had me in stitches, even before he opened his mouth. He was such a clown! I was terribly saddened to see that a leading Irish auctioneer failed to get a higher bid than €40.00 for a work of Leo's called *Churchill and de Gaulle*.

I remember Leo showing me a copy he had made of one of van Gogh's many paintings of sunflowers. 'Better than van Gogh, don't you think?' he said. He had stopped laughing and I realized that he was, in fact, half-serious!

A photo of Samuel Jessurun de Mesquita, in happier times. Samuel's pet name was Sampie. This photo of a smiling Sampie was taken by his brother, Joseph.

Further Reading:

SNOWY OWL
Ulchabhán Sneachtúil

Gabriel Rosenstock

"Gabriel Rosenstock is one of the most original, untypical and inventive writers/thinkers/poets in the world."

World Haiku Review

Gabriel Rosenstock in Paunar Ashram, Wardha, India, an ashram founded by Vinoba Bhave, a disciple of Gandhi, for the spiritual advancement of women. In Paunar, women dedicate their lives to rishi kheti, farming with simple tools, without the help of bullocks, and spinning cloth. The memoirs of Vinoba Bhave are called Moved by Love and in it he says, wisely: 'Without women, men alone cannot bring about world peace which is the crying need of our present times.' Amen.

Other Haiku & Senryu Titles of Interest

Give Me Your Hand
(ISBN: 9781068540837)
Haiku for children 8–13+ with an
international gallery of engaging artwork

"Creates an immersive experience that lingers long after reading."

Iliyana Stoyanova, Blithe Spirit,
Journal of the British Haiku Society, Vol. 35, No.3

LONELINESS
Uaigneas
Gabriel Rosenstock

Loneliness
(ISBN: 9781739561048)
Haiku for children 8–13+ with an
international gallery of superb artwork

"The haiku in this collection are contemplative, sometimes whimsical, and invite readers to find companionship in the smallest moments of existence."

Iliyana Stoyanova, Blithe Spirit,
Journal of the British Haiku Society, Vol. 35, No.3

Fluttering Their Way Into My Head
(ISBN: 9781782010883)
An exploration of haiku for young readers

Tea wi the Abbot
(ISBN: 9780993421754)
Bilingual selection of haiku by John McDonald, in Scots and Irish

Snow / Sneachta: the snow haiku of Issa
(ISBN: 9780995622531)

A Sweater for the Tayfel
Bilingual haiku in response to
artwork by Issacher Ber Rybek
(Ukraine)
(Buttonhook Press, 2022)

Eye of the Fish
Bilingual haiku in response
to photographs by
Debiprasad Mukherjee
(Buttonhook Press, 2023)

Popocatépetl
(ISBN: 9780893044497)
Haiku for readers 8-12+ with an
international gallery of stupendous
artwork

www.ingramcontent.com/pod-product-compliance
Lightning Source LLC
Chambersburg PA
CBHW061230070526
44584CB00030B/4060